I Love You

More Than

BEER

I Love You

More Than

BEER

AND 99 MORE DECLARATIONS OF A GUY'S ADORATION

by Rex Hamilton

with Cathy Hamilton

Andrews McMeel
Publishing, LLC
Kansas City • Sydney • London

Andrews McMeel Publishing, LLC
an Andrews McMeel Universal company
1130 Walnut Street, Kansas City, Missouri 64106
www.andrewsmcmeel.com

10 11 12 13 14 WKT 10 9 8 7 6 5

ISBN: 978-0-7407-5474-6

Library of Congress Control Number: 2005921824

I Love You

More Than

BEER

1.

I love you

more than

BEER.

You taste better than beer (even those pricey microbrews). You're less filling. And when I've had more of you than the law should allow, I can still drive.

2.

I love you
more than

GOLF.

You're more fun to hold than the sweetest putter. I can score with you, even in bad weather. And you'd never penalize me for slow play.

3.

I love you
more than

MONDAY NIGHT FOOTBALL.

You always let me complete my passes (well, almost always) and never break for a commercial just when the action gets good. And I don't have to wait all week for you to thrill me.

4.

I love you
more than

MY CAR.

You take me places I never dreamed I could go. You don't need me to wash you (but I'm still willing, of course!). And I'd never trade you in for a newer model.

5.

♥

I love you
more than

MY DREAM
CAR.

You're softer than the richest Corinthian leather. When your motor's running, you purr like a kitten. And I have no trouble handling your curves.

6.

I love you
more than

MEAT.

You are prime, yet you won't raise my cholesterol. You're rare and well-done at the same time. And you go perfectly with red *or* white wine.

7.

I love you
more than

MY
COMPUTER.

u never give me an error message or make me reboot. I don't
nd buying you new software. And, thankfully, you won't be
solete in five years.

8.

♥

I love you
more than

MY TOOLS.

You feel better in my hands than my best cordless screwdriver. You ain't broke, so I never have to fix you. And when you need recharging, all I have to do is leave you alone.

9.

♥

I love you
more than

THE LAWN.

You look just as nice in the fall as you do in the spring. You're never rough around the edges. And there's no question you're the most lush on the block!

10.

I love you
more than

POKER NIGHT.

You smell much better than cheap cigars. I'd rather stay up all night with you than a bunch of belching guys. And there's no bigger jackpot than the one I hit with you!

I love you
more than

COLLEGE
BASKETBALL.

---

ou've got more moves than a power forward. I can let my uard down with you and still win. And when we go one on one, u never cry "Foul."

12.

I love you
more than

JAMES BOND
MOVIES.

You've got romance, adventure, and plenty of action. I don't
have to worry about you going over to the other side. And at the
end of our chase scenes, you don't explode.

13.

♥

I love you
more than

VICTORIA'S SECRET COMMERCIALS.

You don't need wings to look like an angel. You're the sexiest woman on earth in lace or terry cloth. And even I know that high heels and pajamas are a stupid idea.

14.

I love you
more than

MY FAVORITE
TORN T-SHIRT.

You're softer than 100 percent cotton. You're always clean and pressed and never stained. And when *you* cling to my beer belly, I don't look fat.

15.

♥

I love you
more than

MY ALMA
MATER.

You've taught me more than any professor. I'll always be loyal
to you, no matter what your win-loss record is. And no matter
how old I get, I'll always be your big man on campus.

16.

I love you
more than

MY DRINKING BUDDIES.

You'd never beg me to have "just one more." You wouldn't give me a hard time for going home early. And it only takes one or two rounds to get you tipsy.

17.

♥

I love you
more than

THE REMOTE.

You never get lost between the sofa cushions. I always know where to find you. And when I push all the right buttons of yours, it's a lot more fun than must-see TV.

18.

I love you
more than

MY GARAGE.

You're warm in the winter and cool in the summer. You never get smelly just before trash day. And I never have to clean up your antifreeze spills.

19.

I love you
more than

THE STOCK MARKET.

ven when you're down, your value to me couldn't be higher. I
ove the way you manage your assets. And with you, I get divi-
ends every single day.

20.

♥

I love you
more than

FISHING.

You smell ever so much better than bait. A nibble from you is better than a bite from the biggest catfish. And now that I've caught you, I'm never going to release you.

21.

♥

I love you
more than

THE SUPER
BOWL.

You've got more moves than the flashiest halftime show. You never stop the action for a TV timeout. And I'd much rather spend four and a half hours in the dead of winter scoring with you.

22.

I love you
more than

THANKSGIVING DINNER.

You're more succulent than the juiciest turkey, sweeter than grandma's pumpkin pie. And after extra helpings of you, I don't have to take a nap. (Well, maybe sometimes!)

23.

♥

I love you
more than

NASCAR.

You get my engine running just by walking into the room. You never hurry me when I need to make a pit stop. And I'd never get dizzy watching you do laps.

24.

♥

I love you
more than

SUPERMAN.

Your wit is faster than a speeding bullet. Your touch is more powerful than a locomotive. And when I'm with you, I feel like I'm able to leap tall buildings in a single bound.

♥

I love you
more than

MY
BARBECUE
GRILL.

It doesn't take charcoal or propane to get you smokin'. I love it when you're cooking nice and slow. And I can stand real close to you and never get burned.

I love you
more than

MY
RECLINER.

You make me more comfortable than my favorite chair. I can kick back and relax with you and never feel guilty. And I'd rather fall asleep in your arms than sitting up, drooling on my shirt.

27.

♥

I love you
more than

COFFEE.

You give me a buzz, not a jolt. Your aroma is heaven to my nostrils. And nothing perks me up more than having you in the morning.

28.

♥

I love you
more than

HAMBURGERS.

You're juicy and meaty. Your buns are soft, never stale. And you don't need a lot of condiments to be tasty.

29.

♥

I love you
more than

VACATION.

A day alone with you is like a week on a tropical island. You're my favorite form of R & R. And I don't need a passport to gain entry into your arms.

30.

I love you
more than

THE DOG.

You're a faithful, loyal companion and, truly, my best friend.
You're always eager to show how much you love me. And, best
of all, you don't drool or leave hair all over the couch.

31.

♥

I love you
more than

MY NEWSPAPER.

ou keep me informed and up-to-date. You're funnier than the
mics page. And I don't get my hands dirty when I handle you.

32.

♥

I love you
more than

WORKING OUT.

You can pump me up with your smile. You increase my heart rate just by holding my hand. And I'd rather burn calories huffing and puffing with you any day of the week.

33.

♥

I love you
more than

HALLOWEEN.

You're sweeter than my favorite candy. I like your tricks almost as much as your treats. And you don't need a costume to be a hit with me (in fact, the less costume, the better!).

34.

I love you
more than

MY
BIRTHDAY.

You make me feel younger with each passing year. I don't have
to worry about being "over the hill" with you. And I'd rather
unwrap you than any gift from the mall.

35.

♥

I love you
more than

THE *SPORTS ILLUSTRATED* SWIMSUIT EDITION.

---

don't have to wait until February to get a peek of your skin.
d rather look at you on the beach than a bunch of airbrushed
per models. And you can't snuggle up with a magazine on a
ld winter's night.

36.

I love you
more than

TWINS.

One of you is better than two of anything. You never give me any doubletalk. And, let's face it, I wouldn't know what to do with two women anyway.

37.

♥

I love you
more than

McDONALD'S.

You're more delicious than a Big Mac, saltier than a box of fries. And you know that a happy meal doesn't necessarily end with a toy prize.

38.

I love you
more than

MY TIVO.

I can watch and record your every move in my mind. You can
pause for a bathroom break and pick up right where you left off.
And I never miss a moment of excitement when you're around.

39.

♥

I love you
more than

MY STEREO.

Your voice is music to my ears. You sound lovely, even at high volume. And I love your woofers every bit as much as your tweeters.

40.

I love you
more than

THE
BASEMENT.

You're never dank and hardly ever dark. When a storm approaches, I'd much rather find shelter in your arms. And don't have to mop you up after a big rain.

41.

I love you
more than

DIRT.

---

never mind when you get all over my clothes. You clean up better than anyone I've ever seen. And I don't have to wash after getting my hands on you.

42.

I love you
more than

FIRE.

Your personality is the brightest spark in my life. Your body is hotter than a raging inferno. Our flames of passion will never burn out.

43.

♥

I love you
more than

MONEY.

You're warmer and softer than cold, hard cash. I never need to change you into smaller bills. And the rate of inflation will never diminish your value to me.

44.

I love you
more than

THE GREAT OUTDOORS.

You're as fresh as the clean mountain air. As long as you're in view, the scenery is spectacular. And I never have to check for ticks after frolicking with you.

45.

I love you
more than

ESPN.

You never have a losing season. Your stats are impressive. And when I want an instant replay of Saturday's action, all I have to do is rewind my mind.

46.

♥

I love you
more than

LEATHER UPHOLSTERY.

You're soft and supple and interestingly textured. You're genuine, never faux. And no animals had to die to bring you to me.

47.

♥

I love you
more than

SHARPER
IMAGE.

Your back rubs feel better than a top-of-the-line massage chair. You light up a room better than a solar-powered library lamp. And you're more beautifully engineered than a motorized tie rack.

48.

I love you
more than

ICE CREAM.

Your kisses are more delicious than Rocky Road. Your skin is smoother than French Silk Vanilla. And you don't give me brain freeze when I take you in too quickly.

49.

I love you
more than

OLD
WESTERNS.

You're always one of the good guys (even when you're bad!).
I'd love to have a showdown with you at high noon. And if you
ever showed up in chaps and a white hat, I'd slap my knee and
holler "Yee haw!"

50.

I love you
more than

TEN-YEAR-OLD SINGLE MALT SCOTCH.

You're smoky yet smooth; not too heavy, not too light. And you're best when savored slowly after dinner.

♥

I love you
more than

THE AUTO SHOW.

You're more exciting than the latest concept cars, sleeker than the sportiest roadster. And there's no chance of sticker shock with you because you're priceless.

52.

I love you
more than

PIZZA.

You've got just enough sauce and not too much cheese. You deliver the goods fresh—on time every time. And you're just as hot in the morning as you were the night before.

53.

♥

I love you
more than

MY RUNNING SHOES.

You're sturdy yet flexible. You can handle any terrain with style and comfort. And I can always depend on you to go the distance with me.

54.

♥

I love you
more than

THE BEACH.

You're more spectacular than a sunset over the ocean. The sound of you breathing soothes me more than waves lapping at the shore. And I'd rather feel you in my arms than warm sand between my toes.

I love you
more than

MY CELL
PHONE.

You never interrupt me when I'm trying to have a good time (well, almost never!). I can talk to you and still drive safely. And you never make shrill, annoying sounds in restaurants.

56.

$\mathscr{I}$ *love you*
more than

BOWLING.

Being with you is more thrilling than rolling the perfect game.
No matter how wide we're split, I've still got love to spare. And
you don't make me wear special shoes to roll around with you.

I love you
more than

THE
INTERNET.

You're easy to navigate and delightful to search. I'm never annoyed when you pop up unexpectedly. And when I try to get some place with you, you don't tell me to "shut down and try later." (Well, maybe sometimes.)

58.

I love you
more than

MY HAIR.

You're soft and well behaved, never unruly. You're never too thin on top or long around the ears. And you don't need a drawer full of products to look like a million bucks.

59.

I love you
more than

CHEER-
LEADERS.

You've got more moves than the Laker Girls. You don't need to shake your pom-poms to get my attention. And you never try to get me off the couch by yelling "Go! Go! Go!"

60.

I love you
more than

MOTOR-
CYCLES.

I'd rather have your fingers than the wind in my hair any day. You're the person I was born to be wild with. And you don't make me wear a helmet when I want to get my thrills with you.

61.

♥

I love you
more than

MY
PAYCHECK.

You're more reliable than automatic deposit. Your love is better than money in the bank. And there's no better social security than my future with you.

62.

I love you
more than

NAPS.

You renew and refresh me every time you smile. You're my favorite afternoon delight. And after two hours in your arms, I'm always bright-eyed and bushy-tailed.

63.

♥

I love you
more than

SKIING.

ou're more exhilarating than shushing down a double-
iamond run. When my life is going downhill, you always give
e a lift. And if I start to career out of control with you, I'm in
danger of hitting a tree.

64.

I love you
more than

DINNER.

You're more elegant than a gourmet meal at a five-star restaurant. You comfort me more than my mom's meatloaf and gravy. And if I feast on you late at night, you won't give me heartburn.

65.

I love you
more than

TRAINS.

You're steamier than *The Little Engine That Could*. You never get offtrack when the terrain gets rough. And you have the cutest caboose I've ever seen.

66.

I love you
more than

HOOTERS.

You're hotter than the spiciest buffalo wings and more refreshing than a pitcher of cold beer. And if I wanted "delightfully tacky and unrefined," I wouldn't be here with you.

67.

♥

I love you
more than

THE
HARDWARE
STORE.

Whenever I need to fix a problem, you've always got just the thing to make it right. You've got nuts-and-bolts sense and steely resolve. And you never put the hammer to me when I screw up.

68.

I love you
more than

BASEBALL CAPS.

You make me feel great, even when my hair is looking gnarly.
You always look good, even on a bad-hair day. And with you, I
feel like a kid again.

69.

I love you
more than

CAMPING.

I rather gaze at you than stare up at the stars. You keep me warmer than a goose-down sleeping bag. And when I want s'more of you, all I have to do is say "please."

70.

I love you
more than

THE WEATHER CHANNEL.

No matter what the forecast, you're always the sunshine of my life. You're more reliable than live Doppler radar. And when your front approaches, I never run for cover.

71.

I love you
more than

CHRISTMAS.

You're more fun in the morning than opening presents. You're my favorite thing to find under the mistletoe. And I'd much rather get my jollies with you than with some fat guy in a fuzzy red suit.

72.

I love you
more than

MY SWEATS.

Your arms feel snug but not binding around my neck and waist. You're casual yet sporty. And when you make me too hot the last thing I want to do is peel you off of me.

73.

I love you
more than

BARBECUE.

You're succulent and saucy, smoky and sweet. Your aroma fills up my senses and makes my mouth water. And you're delicious with a pitcher of cold beer and a side of fries.

74.

I love you
more than

MY
HIGH SCHOOL
DAYS.

With you, I'm never a nerd—always one of the studs. Every night with you feels like the prom. And you'd never give me a wedgie for taking too much time in the bathroom.

♥

I love you
more than

BEEF JERKY.

You always give me something to chew on. You're salty and satisfying. And I can count on you to give me sustenance when I'm running low.

76.

I love you
more than

THE
SIMPSONS.

You've got more brains than Lisa. You're more huggable than Maggie. And even on your worst days, you've got way better hair than Marge.

77.

I love you
more than

ROAD TRIPS.

You're more fascinating than a historic marker. I don't have to stop and ask directions when I'm navigating you. And in our intimate moments, you never ask me "How many more minutes?"

78.

I love you
more than

POOL.

I was totally snookered from the first moment I met you. I never have to hustle you to get a good game. And I love to put a little English on you every chance I get.

79.

I love you
more than

BOXING.

You float like a butterfly but never sting like a bee. You always dazzle me with your fancy footwork. And I'd go fifteen rounds with you any night of the week.

80.

I love you
more than

HEAVY
MACHINERY.

You're subtler than a bulldozer, more graceful than a crane
And just being with you is always an earth-moving experience.

♥

I love you
more than

THREE-DAY
WEEKENDS.

very day with you is like a national holiday. You're more fun
han a day off with pay. And there's nothing I'd rather do than
eep through the alarm with you at my side.

I love you
more than

ROCK 'N' ROLL.

You're headier than heavy metal, sexier than rhythm and blues. And I'll be your number-one groupie until the end of the road.

83.

♥

I love you
more than

BASEBALL.

You're my favorite great American pastime. I never have to worry about striking out when you throw me a fast one. And I'd never get upset when the game with you goes into extra innings.

84.

I love you
more than

A ONE-HOUR MASSAGE.

Just being with you is the essence of deep relaxation. You give me tingles just by touching my arm. And you don't charge me $90 at the end of a session with you.

85.

I love you
more than

HUNTING.

---

don't have to get up before dawn to have a sporting chance with you. When I get you in my sights, it's always a rush. And don't have to wear camouflage clothes to catch you.

86.

I love you *more than*

MY MOTHER'S COOKING.

You're sweeter than Mom's apple pie, softer than her home-made rolls. You don't make me clean my plate or eat all of my vegetables. And I can have two or three helpings of you and never get indigestion.

87.

♥

I love you
more than

DOUGHNUTS.

u're sweeter than sugar sprinkles, more luscious than a
eam-filled Danish. And I can enjoy you every morning of the
eek without worrying about getting fat.

88.

I love you
more than

FANTASY
FOOTBALL.

You've always been my top draft pick. You're in a league of
your own. And no matter what my point total, I only want
score with you.

89.

I love you
more than

ICE HOCKEY.

You drive toward your goals with speed and gusto. You never send me to the penalty box for illegal contact. And you know how to handle me without bloodying my nose.

90.

I love you
more than

FINE WINE.

You're not too dry, not too sweet and the perfect complement to any meal. You're aged to perfection—ready to enjoy now and for years to come.

91.

I love you
more than

THE AUTO PARTS STORE.

You're more thrilling than an aisle full of gaskets. You're warmer than a case of antifreeze. And you always have the parts that I desire.

92.

I love you
more than

A TOP-SHELF
MARTINI.

You shake and stir me all at once. No matter how rocky things get, you're always straight up. You can be dry, sweet, or fruity, but I like you best when you're a little dirty.

93.

♥

I love you
more than

MASHED
POTATOES.

You're tasty and buttery-smooth yet you won't clog my arteries. You're the perfect complement to fried chicken, pork chops, and pot roast. And, best of all, you're carb-free.

I love you
more than

THE
OLYMPICS.

I've carried a torch for you for a long, long time. When I won you over, I took the gold. And we don't have to wait every four years to let the games begin!

95.

♥

I love you
more than

A GOOD
CIGAR.

You're well constructed and perfectly wrapped. Your fragrance is not too strong, not too mild. And after a long day, there's nothing like sitting back and relishing you nice and slowly.

96.

I love you
more than

PLAYBOY
MAGAZINE.

You're prettier than the pictures. More stimulating than the, er, articles. And you don't have any of those distracting staples in your stomach.

I love you
more than

FIREWORKS.

ou light up my nights like a Roman candle. Being with you is
 bigger blast than a cherry bomb. And you have a nice long
use so you'll never blow up in my face.

98.

I love you
more than

VIDEO GAMES.

You're fun, challenging, and interactive. Fooling around with you is good for my hand-eye coordination. And I could amuse myself with you for hours and never get a cramp in my thumb.

99.

I love you
more than

A SWISS
ARMY KNIFE.

You were designed for precision, strength, and good looks. You're always sharp, no matter what kind of stuff you have to cut through every day. And I'd never want to find myself on a desert island without you at hand.

100.

I love you
more than

SEX.

You're titillating, hot, and one of life's greatest pleasures. You fulfill my most basic human desire. And I could go days—even weeks—without sex, but I wouldn't survive three minutes without you.